BOOKL

Photographs by Thomas Haywood

Poems by

Patricia Ace
Sujata Bhatt
Sarah Jackson
Sam Meekings
Mary Palmer
Richard Price
David Troupes

Also by Knucker Press:

Light & Dark
The Scarecrow
Inextinguishable
Way Out
Head To Head
Twinset

First published in 2009 by Knucker Press
in association with Polwarth Publishing.

Edited and designed by Jane McKie

Typeset in 10pt Sabon by 3btype.com

ISBN: 978-0-9555013-6-4

www.knuckerpress.com

Acknowledgements

Sujata Bhatt's poem 'Faux Fable, with Butterfly' first appeared in *Ploughshares* (USA).

Sarah Jackson's poems 'Aristotle's Lantern' and 'The Yard' first appeared in her pamphlet, *Milk* (Pighog Press).

'Call em Lanthorn Jaws & Bitches' is a quote from John Clare's 'To a Methodist Parson'.

The italicised line in 'Cattle Songs' on page 71 is quoted from the poem 'Waking in Winter' by Sylvia Plath.

Booklight is dedicated to the memory of

Mary Palmer

18 June 1957 – 9 June 2009

Contents

WHERE IS YOUR SILVER DREAM?

Sujata Bhatt

THE CAVE OF THE HEART

Patricia Ace

CALL EM LANTHORN JAWS & BITCHES

Sarah Jackson

NECROPOLIS
Sam Meekings

LANDLIGHT
David Troupes

ILLUMINATIONS
Mary Palmer

NON-REFLECTIVE GLASS
Richard Price

BIOGRAPHIES

Where is your Silver Dream?

Sujata Bhatt

Always Choose the Jack of Hearts

Always choose the jack of hearts, my friend.

The king is blind, the queen is cold,
        and the ace is full of lies.

But the jack of hearts
        knows the way.

The jack of hearts can speak
        with worm-light
and crushed butterflies.

*

Does your soul have chromosomes too?

And a few broken cells?

What colour? What colour?

You'll never know.

Can your soul really be
        a butterfly?

Gregor's Sister Speaks

Gregor, dear brother,
why didn't you think of wings?

Why didn't you turn into a butterfly instead?

I would have joined you, and mother and father too—
        if only you had told us how.

We could have all grown huge orange wings,
you could have added tiger stripes
        to be different—

We could have made the sky
orange and gold with black tiger lines
                brushing against the clouds.

We could have inspired lilies to grow as tall as trees—

And the neighbours would have called us the new angels—

We could have flown far away
        migrating to India or Costa Rica—

We could have escaped our fate,
                our ordinary deaths—
truly escaped what History expected from us.

A Word Spoken on Land

A word spoken on land
    is worth nothing at sea—

It's a meaningless, dangerous sound,
        he's told.

So the sailor turns mute
    as the ship sails south—

Then, in a new land he has never seen,
    he watches butterflies;
catches two of them to bring back
    to his treeless island—

Little nymphs he won't set free.

'What shall I name you?'
        He asks—

'What shall I name you?'

She Flies High

She flies high, this Malaysian Tree Nymph—

White wings translucent with black loops—

Snow leopard spots—

Pale greyish white
with black spots, and veins dusted black—
Yes, black dusted.

Higher and higher, she flies close to the treetops—
A lost scarf, a lost ribbon
        carried away by the wind—

Rice paper,
        paper kite tree nymph—

and the snow leopard design on her wings
        opens and opens—

Soul of a leopard.

*

We say she's full of kindness;
we say she's elegant and able
        to speak with trees.

But maybe she's not.
Maybe she's bitter and mean,
simply oozing with viciousness,
waiting to grow back into a leopard—

And now, watch her resting on a leaf,
                    wings erect,
and then, hanging upside down, her wings
gathered together like ruffles on a skirt
Audrey Hepburn might have worn—

The Tired Butterfly

The tired one we saw—
a butterfly— that swallowtail tiger
we saw hovering over black soil—

Not a flower in sight.

Was it dying? Or was it just drowsy?
Was it famished? Why so lethargic?

Not a flower in sight, just a vast lawn—

Vast lawns and tall trees,
and the light waiting for Edward Hopper—

No Tiger is Plain

No tiger is plain—

Even you,
Plain Tiger Butterfly,
          are not plain.

Creature of the blazing sun,
can we avoid your poison?

Ignored by birds and lizards,
you burn in the fields,
surviving everything.

Where is Your Silver Dream?

Scarlet and male and Mormon—

Why Mormon?

Is Eros so new, so American?

The God of Love craves eggs.

Sappho would have found you.

You used to be a tall girl
        with dark hair.
You used to wear a silver necklace
        with that red dress.

Where is your silver dream?

Where is your love, the dragonfly,
from whom you have stolen so much?

You Have the Blue

'You have the blue I want,'
he said, 'and I'll kill you for it.'

And he did.
He killed and took the blue
from a thousand butterflies—

And he rubbed the blue into his skin
everywhere—   slowly, slowly—
        especially on his face—

And he swallowed what he could
even though it was metallic
with a dizzy, glittering light—

But the magic had gone,
the power had gone to the Lord of Death,
who arrived promptly and took him away
despite his efforts to reach blueness.

Oblique

Oblique, gentle—
a fluttering near your peripheral vision—

First, she powdered her eyelids
until they shimmered like butterflies—

Butterflies in the sun,
        early in the morning.

The story you tell defines you—

Will you add lilacs, will there be butterflies?

How many birds will be allowed
        to interrupt your voice?

Will the butterflies be white or blue,
        orange or yellow?

Plain white, or just orange and ordinary?

Can a butterfly be ordinary?

The story you tell defines you—
Will there be butterflies?

And if there are butterflies,
        who will be the first to see them?

At First She was a Butterfly

At first she was a butterfly
        my daughter,
the way I felt her within me—

And then she grew into a fish,
a strong swimmer from the start—

But I hold on to the first day
        I felt her move,
a small butterfly touching flower after flower—

Long Yellow Dresses

Three girls chase butterflies
        across the garden—

Back and forth they sprint in their long yellow dresses,
        dresses with purple ribbons—

Back and forth—
        how their long flaxen hair flies,

and now their braids begin to unravel,
        their fine hair soon to be tangled

as they toss their heads against the light,
        against the wind—

It's freedom they're after—
freedom contained in the slant of the light—

They've just finished their dance lessons—
        or have they run away?

It's the chasing they like—
they don't want to hurt the butterflies—

And they're not sure
they want the butterflies to touch them.

Faux Fable, with Butterfly

Sky, cloudless.
Light, unhampered as it falls across the mountains,
across the lake, across the trees surrounding the lake.
Day after day, a woman watches this light
move across the landscape.
In her story, the hero sails away, saddened, angry—
while the light casts harsh shadows.
The hero is never seen again.
Everyone speaks of the lake in her story,
wrongly assuming the hero has drowned.
Even though the title of her story is 'Butterfly'.
Singular. Solitary. One butterfly.
No one pays attention.
Yet, there is one butterfly;
one butterfly the heroine follows
through the woods for hours,
even though the woods are full of wild boars
and archers, handsome archers she would prefer not to meet;
still, the heroine is not deterred.
How she gasps as the butterfly settles on a log
and opens its dark wings, blue and blue-violet.
The light suddenly caught by those wings,
caught by hunger, by love, by urgent need—
by a need so urgent, the light is caught unawares.
Even though there is a butterfly, huge—
the wings, sheer petals with fine veins, almost like skin,
moist, quivering, drinking in the light—

while the body at the centre, the deep, deep brown
pretends to sleep, each sheath of hair resting,
engulfed in its own dream—
Even though there is a butterfly, huge—
the wings drinking in the light—
a flash of colours—
no one sees it. Everyone is blind to it;
everyone speaks of the lake instead,
not knowing that the lake is an ornament,
a backdrop for the hero
who is actually searching for that butterfly,
that blue-violet butterfly, hidden
to all, except, of course, to the heroine;
the heroine who is quiet and knows
where to look. Remember, the heroine is a daughter
who rejects her mother's bitterness. She refuses
to inherit such anger, such bitterness.
Meanwhile, the light is generous
to the mountains and to the lake,
generous to the trees and the flowers,
as if knowing that always
a butterfly's wings will reshape it—
prisms restructured with such hunger—

The Cave of the Heart

Patricia Ace

The Homecoming

For all I'd waited a score of years for his return,
when he came back to Ithaca he wasn't the same man.
Leaving aside that ridiculous disguise, he'd changed.
Even the poor old dog's heart gave out in fright
at the sight of him.
                    Having wowed us all with his archery
skills, there was the inevitable bloodbath; my rapacious
suitors put to the sword, the twitching soles of my twelve
little maids, who'd been like sisters to me, strung up
by their necks like the spoils of a hunt, as if he still
had something to prove.
Yes, you could call it a period of readjustment.

We need to talk I told him. I'd heard the rumours
about him and the witch but at least he had the sense to admit it.
She'd borne him three sons by the time he realised he missed me.
And I'd spent three years unravelling each night, unpicking
stitches from that pointless shroud until my fingers bled;
my fingertips thickened like a man's, until they grew too rough,
too clumsy for delicate work like sewing or repair.

We learned to rub along okay in public.
Well, everybody likes a happy ending and we still had a lot
in common, we'd always been like-minded.
During the daytime it was fine.
                                But at night it was another story.
The sheets drenched with sweat. Him waking pale and quaking
from his dream. Always the same dream.
                                          Back in the cave
on that well-wooded isle; the monstrous ogre with his single eye,
maw swilling with human blood, beard caked with his grim fodder,
saying *Don't worry, my friend, my Nobody, I will eat you last of all.*

The Speleologist

I've never been afraid of the dark
or small spaces. Between a rock
and a hard place holds no fear for me.
My mother was a firm believer
in swaddling, routine.
My birth had nearly killed her.
Untimely ripped my mother quoted,
Out the sunroof my father quipped.

As a boy I made a den in the coal shed.
I loved the smell of it – mineral, earthy.
A tang of iron, something I remembered
from burying my head in my mother's lap.
My Dad bought me a boiler suit, a head torch.
That boy'll be a miner, he smiled. *Or a bin man*,
said my mother, *Look at the state of him!*

In my teens I watched hours of films
about submarines.
I spent a whole weekend just going up
and down in a lift.

At home I keep the curtains drawn
and the heating off, forget to fix the washer
on that dripping tap.

Stump Cross

I negotiate petrified
limestone channels
like something being passed,
a molecule of food,
an egg through a tube.

Alkali droplets gaze
from the vault like fish-eyes,
cling to ridged icicles
the colour of bruises –
moss, ochre, bone, rust.

Here I see a serrated
sheep's jaw, there an elephant's
furrowed leg. Lace curtains,
snowdrift, batwings.

All life here by proxy
slowly forming drip by drip.
Antlers, sandcastles,
organ pipes, lips.

The Spark

deep in the cave of the heart
a spark
deep in the dark of the heart
a breath
coaxes the flame of the spark
a light
candle in the temple
thought
tabernacle of stories
beat
come from the sound of a gong
a dance
clash between light and dark
a word
mined from the seams of the cave
alive
deep in the dark of the heart
a flame
deep in the cave of the heart
a spark

The Marriage

the nights I've wept alone
in the silent empty house

how love has come again
when I didn't know it could

you think you've lost some jewel
but it turns up in your sheets

I could smell him in the gloom
as a bat senses predator or prey

taste the salt of his sweat
feel his body warm as stone
heated by the sun all day

a voice came out of blackness
Is it you, my Queen?

*

this man takes my hand
holds it to his heart

pulls me into darkness
his tongue between my lips

my thighs around his hips
my nails press on his spine

the wind licking the cave mouth
a tremolo of thunder

a hundred butterflies beat their wings
the sound from out our mouths

lightning striking home
a cloudburst on the plain

the valley fully flooded
the rivers all in spate

The Burden

I walked all day with the bundle shawled in sacking,
heavier in my arms than it had been in my belly,
its mewling stoppered at last by motion and milk,
its face smooth as a stone tumbled by the tide.

What a thirst I had! My lips chapped and cracked
as my ebony nipples. Each hour that passed marked
by the tug of my breasts, which swelled and hardened,
smarted as they rubbed the rough cloth of my dress.

We reached the cave at sunset, my feet tattooed in blood,
some dried, some fresh from the rocky ascent. I slaked
my tongue in the cave's cold pool until it filled like a sponge;
plunged my feet in, washed the blood from between my legs.

I thought to leave my burden then but its eyes flickered
open and at its first feeble cries, a stain appeared at my breast.
I pinched my teat to its mouth, tried not to look but
its stare pulled me back, my womb pulsing hard as it drank.

When its head lolled from sucking, sated at last, neck slack
as a wet rag, a pearly dribble glistened on its cheek – peaceful
at least. I niched it in a nook of rock, all feeling gone
from my fingers, my feet, grateful for the numbing cold,

and walked out onto the windless hillside, shadows stark
and silent, the sky's million witnesses blinking at my shame.

Call em Lanthorn jaws & bitches

Sarah Jackson

Aristotle's Lantern

You are a sea-urchin, legless,
as you slide along the blue-rimmed
pool-side to the shallow-end
where I'm untangling my goggles.
Ducking up and under, your white cap
is a beacon; when you smile
I see your small hollow teeth.

I tell you I've had this awful cold
for weeks; that's why I haven't called
for quite some time. You won't listen:
Really Mother, you say,
pulling yourself out of the water,
removing your swimming cap.
You've dyed your hair brown again.

I hug you back – all arms and legs –
try to pretend we are not naked
but for the blue and black lycra
strapped to our backsides, our chests.
I notice my knuckles,
yellow and globby like fungi,
clutching the silver steps.

When you kiss me again I look away,
watch water-ants run down my skin.
You touch my hand: *What is it, Mother?*
Only I cannot say that when you move in
to kiss me, you drip water on my face
as if from a rice spoon, and I'm afraid
I will bite out your tongue if we speak.

Taggart's Garden

I'm inside, despite the gates:
roaming the Aciphylla bank,
the Meconopsis bed.

White wrought iron benches
line the upper terrace
like the skeletons of dogs;

no one comes in winter.
I think of James Taggart
sinking frost-tender shrubs,

in the gully of Meikle burn
whittling borders, lodging bamboo,
all that earth in his thumbs.

Behind the long pond,
a pignut hickory crowds
an empty red hut,

filling it out like a shout.
I cannot bear to leave
this nest of rhododendrons

straddling the sea cliff.
Eucalyptus fingers my cheek,
swamp oaks bend in the wind.

Security, 10 pm

I'm practically inside this computer
when you turn out the lights.

Passing under the window,
head dipping like a grebe,

your hair glints in the street-lamp.
I'm in a choke of books:

my hard-drive is sweating,
pencils upright like stakes,

and my eyes falling out of my face.
I stop to watch you walk away

wanting to walk with you.
The shape of you turns my skin,

brushing my cheek so softly
I think of a night sparrow.

Now I am out, at large
in night. Moss under my nails,

mud in my teeth, dark climbs
up my legs. Wanting you,

my bare skin breathes.
I have the taste for forest.

The Lotus Eater's Sister

I

She takes me on a Greek-island cruise
insisting we'll have a fabulous time
but I lie on deck, gaping up at clouds

that move in dead-straight lines
and slip my forefinger between my ribs
because that's all the space I know.

She keeps watch over me; her brows
crowbars when she frowns.
For a moment, she reminds me of our father,

then it's gone. But tonight, a North wind
fills our sails, blowing us off-course.
There is the sound of oars.

II

I swim to an island with no name.
Here, it's always dusk, the sun a pinkish glow
like a fat girl's cheek when she runs.

I bask in palm groves, turning my skin
to amber; refuse to see any visitors,
especially the police.

When I wake again, it's white;
the place dotted with natives, smiles pasted
on their faces. I read the names

on their uniforms as they hand me
a jujube petal curled like a white worm
on a petri-dish and tell me, *Eat*;

offer me Lotus wine from a green bottle
like the deepest sea and tell me, *Drink*.
They fix up a supply right by my bed.

The next day, I am crawling.
I suck stamen, crush petals in my teeth,
juice slipping down my throat, filling me up

until the light is in me, all around me
and there's no space left between my ribs.
Please, I don't want to go home.

III

I see my daughter docking. She signs
a clipboard. Their heads are nodding.
Some speak on pink telephones.

I don't open my eyes, knowing already
it's dark when I'm wheeled out,
carried by two girls onto a boat.

My sister smoothes down the blankets
files her nails and watches me
while her big-breasted soldiers

split the grey sea with their oars;
it's only when the moon blinks again
and I feel a North Wind tip the sails

that I creep away to the gallows
to finger the dark growing spaces
between my bones.

The Yard

Afterwards, I move to a one-bed
with a yard: its ratty paving
cluttered with chipped pots

and moss-lined like your stubble;
the broken trellis reminds me
of my fractured elbow that time.

In the flowerbed I dig up tulip bulbs
and think they won't stop;
dream of them at night bubbling up

and down like garden peas in a pan.
I picture babies or your bald head
when we shaved it one spring.

The last tenants left six plastic chairs,
stacked. I put them out on the street
with a polite notice: *Help yourself,*

but no one does. I plant chopsticks
in the flowerbed – rude fingers
to stop the cats from crapping.

I haven't done any laundry for weeks
but I string a washing line anyway,
hang tea lights along it

and so, at night, it's as if someone
is still watching me as I stretch out
on the cold, hard paving slabs.

NECROPOLIS

Sam Meekings

Necropolis

I

What he missed most
was the crackle of leaves
beneath his feet.

Death had unpicked him,
unslipping the cross stitch
along the seams of skin
that knotted flesh to shadow.

And so his shadow
was now all that was left of him –
he was spilt ink,
the last dregs of red
heavy at the bottom of the bottle,
or the kind of midnight ocean
in which clusters of stars
shimmer and bob.

He was the imaginary friend
that has been grown out of.

He was viscous, thick.
The densest, heaviest dark matter
fixes the visible
and the invisible world together,
just as the words
a mother mumbles
beneath her breath
keep the rucksack held tight
on her child's shoulders
on the first day of school.

II

Though we cannot see dark matter,
we might infer its presence
by observing its effects –
as with a gale whisking up leaves
and tumbling clumsily through the tops of trees.

So it is with love. The way
he used to move his hands
almost nervously, teasing
the wedding ring, the way
a blush would sometimes blossom
across his cheek. The invisible
dot on the map
where two hearts meet.

Love is a weight
that tied him to that place,
that house, that chair, that bed.

A shadow is a weight
that tethers a body to the earth;
as he grew he shrank into it.

III

When he tried to move
he found himself
getting tangled in the bracken,
snagged on wiry fences,
mixing and mingling
with the shadows of stray dogs.

He was slippery, wobbly.
He was not taken
with the death of his body.
Surely, he thought, nothing can exist
without its opposite. In the plains
and paddies of rural China
the parents of an unmarried son
will walk for days
between villages
in search of the corpse
of a young woman
to bury beside him.

Because nothing is worse
than venturing into death alone.
If a body cannot be found,
one can be made of straw.
Groom and straw bride
buried side-by-side
while abandoned shadows
are left to measure out
the last of the light.

IV

The Ministry of Shadows
deals in applications, permits,
queries, complaints, tribunals,
disputes and petty claims.

He flitted up to an empty office,
soaring in on the last lash
of a plastic-bag breeze.

There he found a leaflet –
'New arrivals should try not to panic:
with a positive outlook,
eternity need not be as troubling
a concept as it may initially appear,
and the absence
of a corporeal form
need not be cause for alarm
permitted that due care
is paid to the following points...'

v

Our shadows are made first,
knotting us into the sticky dark
of the womb, and already
swelling in the printouts
of the ultrasound.

His was the imaginary friend
always at his back.
It was the shirt that never fit.

His was jittery and long
prancing behind him in the school play,
nervous and drawn close
in the photos of his wedding day.

Shadows are the receptacles
into which our memories our poured,
hot, molten tar and cement.
These are what remain –

the universe crammed full
of dark matter,
the restless memories
of half-forgotten pasts.

VI

He was whipped up
by the wind, frayed at the edges.
He slunk past his old house –
the lights still on,
the sound of a bath running.

The drip of water,
the glow of the television,
the last shirt flapping on the line,
and nothing left
but everything he'd left behind.

VII

His shadow grew longer,
away from the last spools of sun
being stretched across the city.

Warped, bent, tugged
out of shape. His last hours
played on repeat.

He thought of his son.
He thought of his wife.
And watched
light fold under light
sky over sky
and waited for his shadow
to become enveloped
in the overhanging shadows
of the tower block, the walls, the gate –

and in that moment
when his shadow sunk under
the thickness of another,
he remembered
being a child

unknotting school shoes
and pulling off socks
and leaving his life
at the end of the street
and running into the park
to crunch and stomp and shriek –

and what he missed most
was the crackle of leaves
beneath his feet.

THOMAS BENNETT
ALSO THEIR CHILDREN
ELIZABETH
AGED 6 WEEKS
JOSEPH
AGED 7 MONTHS
MARY
ALEXANDER
AGED 3 MONTHS
DAVID
AGED 3 MONTHS
JANE HENDERSON
ROBERT THOMSON BENNETT

Landlight

David Troupes

The Man With the Fine View

Grinds the giddy machinery: the cloud-soured hills,
the bargain bin miles,
the beanpoles
of storm-light billowing.

Thinks of his wife kneeling
in her allotment,
the runner beans plaiting their ladder
of blossom.

Searches for any fortune in the glittering
crease of river, the storm-light distilled
and deep at home in April's
warm palm.

Rolls
as the land rolls, fills
as the wind fills. Her gypsy hoops, her freckled wrists, her worn nails.
Her light. Her salt.

Whitsun

Not fire but silk:
a bolt

of silk unspooling above the wound-
red scratch

of dirt road. A limp of wire fence,
a language

tossed away, strewn
like quick rain.

A dreg
not of wine but milk.

I Walk All Morning Under My Hair Shirt of Skin

The woods are fitting themselves to the winds.
The widows are fitting themselves to their weeds.
The winds are fitting themselves to the wilds.
The weeds are fitting themselves to our words.
The wilds are fitting themselves to the wed.
The words are fitting themselves to these wounds.
The wed are fitting themselves to the wonders.
The wounds are fitting themselves to the woods.
The wonders are fitting themselves to the widows.

The Anvil

A racket of light, a bloom
of rain, a brief
wedge of sun, and the river's

beery stupor.
At 2:57 we round a crook in the trail
and a kestrel flees, threads itself away above the brown

thread of water.
Down
in the melt and slur of fern the young rabbit

with a two-inch wound opened in its side
takes no shelter, screams
like its tongue were peeling from its throat. Man-o-wars

drag their pearl strings of rain
through the kettledrumming north, everything beating itself
on the anvil of everything.

Cattle Songs

I

The cattle work their jaws
under a bone bowl of sky

and snow hills, in this waste of frozen ley,
warmed by winter's wealth of straw.

II

Three head.
I can taste the tin of the sky – the real tin thing.

Ground me, my totems, my three minds,
my little cattle of ley with your one-fifth lead.

III

From rick to rick, shelter to shelter
they walk their leys and their lines, until

unlooked for, unwelcome almost – that first catamenial
melt, that vernal welter.

The Body at Last Gives in

Like thoughts
in the heads
of the granddaddy hills,

each thought itself
thinking
as it chews, chewing as it thinks,

the great
shrunk body
of the hills tipping their hoary chins

to the sea.
The cattle eat. They eat.
The hills are tired.

ILLUMINATIONS

Mary Palmer

Illumination

In 1879 eight arc lights bathed the promenade;
artificial sunshine they called it.

Today one million lights flood the town.

From a splash, an illumination, dreams come into being.

Reflections

'The only time I went to Blackpool, I got stuck
at the top of the Big Wheel with my daughter.
I don't like heights.' Laughter.

Memories, colours, bleed into the sea.

Blackout

A dark sea's hush. During the war,
blackout. The only colour
in hotels and boarding houses,
bulbs painted a Dolly blue.

Now guesthouses are ablaze, lit by neon.

But under this Victorian construct
the same dank smell and salt sand.
A breeding ground.

Streaming

These days, people live so fast they are streams of light.
Tokyo, Las Vegas, Blackpool – the images fuse.
Who are they? Where are they going?
Is there one source of light or many?

It's what we focus on that matters.

Low Tide

In postmodern times, it is said that there is no truth,
only the glitter of a mirror ball, that there are no
foundations.

Here, under the pier's salt soaked boards,
slender pilings hold steady.

NON-REFLECTIVE GLASS

Richard Price

Non-Reflective Glass

I'd lost a ringpull she gave me,
both slaughtered on a glorified traffic island.
There'd been an impromptu engagement –
29th of March but 'still a leap year – answer yes or no.'
I was in a hurry, I'd cut my knuckle on the metal.
'Uh-huh but you'd need to sign a pre-nuptial.'
I dripped blood on her elasticated cuff
but she wouldn't sign my office trousers.
She said she was against self-harm –
personally, she preferred a more distributive philosophy –
she might not marry me now.
"It's not all about you, you know –
could we have a trial,
a trial relationship?"

I lost a drawing she gave me.
Her step-nephew had crayoned a five-piece sequence,
crocuses I think, yellow over the lines,
and red plus blue is how you make purple, conceptually speaking.
He was in his final year at the Royal College of Art,
or it might have been Sandhurst,
and she'd helped him with his maths, with his bible references.

She lost track of me. There had been a year of letters.
She'd wanted to travel to all the territories
        with spring flowers on their stamps,
mail me with her travelogues.
They were personal, holy, she cautioned, but...
could I get them published as widely as possible?,
digitised for a gallery? She'd let me write a preface, or sing.
She'd journeyed first to the Summer Isles but the issuing office there
had long closed,
'This damned archipelago is all seals and scenery.'
Belgium's black flowers looked sinister but it might have been ironic,
art's more important if it's tackling the issues, yeah?
No news for weeks and then Madagascar. 'They
        respect their ancestors here,
by the way. Why did you never respect my ancestors?
They bring the bones out and so on.
All I ever wanted you to do
was respect my ancestors.'

Colour is seldom so close,
but the crocus photographs she dispatched
(why no stamps this time? –
that was a wet walk to the depot
and I was distracted; I didn't appreciate having to bluff my ID)-
but the crocus photographs she dispatched from who knows where
could be 'blooming planets circling up.'
So Ruth-my-sister's-daughter says
(not Stella's Ruth, obviously, is what I'm saying – 'my' Ruth)
and maybe Filmic is right – just eight and some critic –
they weren't flowers at all
but entities somewhere near the improvised edge of the universe,
vast agglomerations of minerals hurtling towards us
made still, made delicate, by distance.

You can't talk cogently through photography,
focus blurs thought,
but I've set her images beneath non-reflective glass,
a gallery in the hall,
and we could talk colour theory, neuroscience, astronomy
at her own private view if she'd just RSVP
or, at least, send some scribble of a crocus,
proof that she has survived another winter
that a certain armour plated flower
          has pierced one more enamelled frost.

Biographies

PATRICIA ACE'S first chapbook of poems, *First Blood*, is published by HappenStance Press. In 2008 she won the poetry section of *Aesthetica's* Creative Works Competition and 3rd Prize in the *Mslexia* Women's Poetry Competition. She also graduated from Glasgow University with an MLitt in Creative Writing for which she was awarded a Distinction. She lives with her partner and two teenage children in Crieff, where she works part-time as a yoga teacher and creative writing tutor.

SUJATA BHATT was born in Ahmedabad, India, and grew up in Pune, India and in the United States. To date, she has published seven collections of poetry with Carcanet Press. The recipient of numerous awards, such as the Commonwealth Poetry Prize (Asia), and the Cholmondeley Award, her latest collection, *Pure Lizard*, was shortlisted for the Forward Prize and received the German Literature Award, Das neue Buch, in 2008. She has translated poetry from Gujarati and German into English. Her work has been widely anthologised, broadcast on radio and television, and has been translated into more than twenty languages. She is a frequent guest at literary festivals throughout the world. Currently, she lives in Germany with her family.

THOMAS HAYWOOD was brought up in the Highlands of Scotland in the small village of Newtonmore. He first picked up an SLR camera when he was 13 years old and is self taught. After school, he worked in the hospitality and agricultural industries. He went to Napier University in Edinburgh and graduated in 2000 with a BA (Hons) in Languages & Export Management. In 2006 he turned to photography professionally. He is also a Great Britain International Baseball Umpire.

SARAH JACKSON lives in Brighton, where she is completing doctoral research in creative and critical writing at Sussex University and working towards her first full collection of poetry. Her pamphlet, *Milk*, which was published by Pighog Press, was shortlisted for the Michael

Marks Poetry Award, and her work features in the anthology, *Voice Recognition: 21 Poets for the 21st Century* (Bloodaxe, 2009). She is the poetry editor for *The New Writer* magazine.

SAM MEEKINGS grew up on the south coast, before studying in Oxford and Edinburgh. Since 2005 he has lived and worked in various parts of China. His first collection of poetry, *The Bestiary*, was published by Polygon in 2008. His first novel, *Under Fishbone Clouds*, will be published by Polygon in 2009.

MARY PALMER spent nine years as an NHS dietitian and took to writing poetry. Worse still – left her job, wrote furiously for two years and surfaced clutching an MA in Creative Writing. Her work has appeared in many magazines and anthologies; it has also been broadcast on radio and satellite TV. She is a seasoned performer of poetry, both in the UK and Europe. Her first collection, *Iona, a story told through poems, prose, quotes and images*, was published in 2008. See www.awenpublications.co.uk for further details.

RICHARD PRICE's poetry collections include *Lucky Day* and *Greenfields* and the forthcoming *Rays*. He has collaborated with several artists on a number of artist's books: with Ronald King (*gift horse* and *little but often*), with Karen Bleitz (*The Mechanical Word*), and with Caroline Isgar (*Wake Up and Sleep*). He has performed and recorded his lyrics as part of the Mirabeau project (www.myspace.com/mirabeauproject) and has his official website at www.hydrohotel.net. His work has been translated into several languages including the selection *Cartas de Ontem*, translated into Portuguese by Virna Teixeira and published in Brazil. He is the Head of Modern British Collections at the British Library, London.

DAVID TROUPES was born and raised in the ferny woods of Massachusetts, moved around quite a bit, and now lives with his wife in West Yorkshire, where he works in social housing. His poetry has appeared in many British and American journals, and Two Ravens Press will publish his first full collection in 2009. Currently he's hard at work writing and illustrating a children's book titled *The Renaming of the Birds*. Pay a visit to www.buttercupfestival.com for more information.

KNUCKER PRESS is a small press dedicated to publishing collaborations where word and image are mutually enriching. Established in 2007, its mission is to match writers with artists to produce high-quality and innovative books and pamphlets. The styles and formats are varied, but all are linked by the strength and sympathy of the artistic partnerships, creating works that are both unique and accessible.

ONE Magazine is an international quarterly from Polwarth Publishing – founded by Martin Belk, Polwarth Publishing is a Scotland-based arts enterprise committed to bringing fresh work forward from new artists and known talent. www.iamone.co.uk